The Essence Of Strategy

Η Πεμπτουσία της Στρατηγικής
La Esencia de la Estrategia
De Essentie van Strategie
L'Essenza della Strategia
Det essientielle i strategi
L'essence de la stratégie
La esenco de strategio
สาระสำคัญของกลยุทธ์
האסטרטגיה מהות
جوهر الاستراتيجية
Суть стратегии
전략 의 본질
戦略の要諦
战略的本质
戰略的本質

Table Of Contents

Foreword 5

Why We Need To Rethink Strategy 7

What Strategy Really Is 15

The Components Of Strategy 25

The Time Nature Of Strategy 31

How To Create Strategy 37

Strategy In Large And Complex Organization 45

The Realpolitik Of Strategy 49

Important Strategic Concepts 55

Advanced Strategy Concepts 61

Relationship Of Strategy To Other Discipline 73

Useful Reference Works 79

Foreword

This book describes what strategy is and how to do it well. You could argue (and in fact I would argue) that strategy is the discipline that sits above all others. Strategy is about how to win; how to succeed. I wrote this book because whilst strategy is incredibly important and powerful, it is almost always poorly understood, defined, articulated and executed.

Strategy is about winning by making smart choices. It applies to companies, governments, individual people, charities, sports teams. Anywhere there are goals and choices to make. Most of the ideas in this book are relevant in all areas of life. This book is concise and dense. It is not an easy-to-use template, workshop or quick fix. It is written in a linear structure, but there are many threads that build on, refer back to, or refine each other. Some of the concepts are in tension with each other – such as increasing choice versus reducing complexity. Therein lies the challenge of strategy.

I recommend reading this book three times. First, quickly and lightly, to get the lay of the land. Second, as if reading a newspaper, getting some facts without much judgement. Thirdly and finally, absorb it, engage with it, debate with it, and develop your own opinions about it.[1]

Finally, bear in mind that meaning is never found purely in the object. Meaning is found in the relationship between subject (you) and object (this book). Hopefully reading this book will unlock and reshape some of your pre-existing knowledge and ideas about strategy.

Enjoy!

---

[1] This idea of reading a text three times is different to, but inspired by G.I. Gurdjieff's "Beelzebub's Tales To His Grandson".

Why We Need To Rethink Strategy

Strategy Saves Us From The Tyranny Of Brute Force

There are only three ways to succeed:
1. Succeeding through brute force. Simply applying the resources we've got to the task at hand.
2. Succeeding through stratagems. Using tactics to trick the opponent.
3. Succeeding through strategy. Making smart, focused choices, to outperform what might be expected of us, given the resources at hand.

In a world of brute force, we simply use what we've got. When we come across a challenge, we 'boil the ocean' – ploughing through the challenge mechanically. If we come across an opponent with more than we have, we lose. If we come across a task that requires more than we have, we fail. A world without strategy is brutal and uninspiring. Adding stratagems – or trickery – to the picture means that sometimes we can achieve more than expected, e.g. by feinting left, then striking right, or by confusing the enemy. Stratagems are limited though, in that they are mostly appropriate in a context where there is an opponent, they are often not repeatable (once the enemy knows our trick), and they are often win-lose rather than win-win.

Strategy, however, has the potential to lift us repeatedly and sustainably from the ugliness of a brute force world, allowing us to achieve much more than would be expected with the resources at hand, and sometimes create win-win, where all participants achieve more than expected.

Strategy Is Everywhere

Because strategy is the discipline of success, about creating focus wherever there are choices, *strategy applies in almost every aspect of life*. Strategy applies to government, public sector and not-for-profit enterprises, just as it does in for-profit enterprises. Strategy applies where there is competition, or an enemy, or where there is not, such as in monopolies or personal life and career planning. Strategy applies to individuals as well as groups. Strategy applies equally to the small and the large, the young and the old, the rich and the poor, the strong and the weak. Strategy is critical both when you are winning and when you are losing.

This means that strategy is *not a luxury*. Some enterprises behave as if strategy is a high-falutin' discipline, only to be indulged in in the good times. Quite the opposite – strategy is even more necessary in the tough times, when resources are constrained.

Strategy Has Become A Punctuation Mark

The word strategy has lost almost all meaning. People put the word strategy next to other words in order to make them sound important, but are not really clear what the word strategy means. In that sense, *strategy has almost stopped being a word*, and become a specialized punctuation mark that imbues the noun before it with importance. This is a shame, because, as discussed above, real strategy is in fact a critical discipline that can make individual entities win, and make the world a happier, more productive place.

Strategy Is Not The Same As Planning

Most organisations and many individuals have plans. A strategy is not the same as a plan. The strategy sets direction, and the plan documents the details of moving in that direction. In a corporate context the strategy sets out how we will win, the capabilities we will need, the principles that will keep us on track. The plan then cements that strategy in a set of projects and programmes, start and finish dates, costs, revenues, risks, people, partners, methods etc.

Plans must be guided by and aligned with strategies, but must be managed as separate artefacts. This becomes very obvious in very volatile times, when plans change very frequently, but the strategy remains as a compass, ensuring we continue to head in our strategic direction. If your strategy changes as fast as your plan, you don't really have a strategy. (The time nature of strategy and planning is discussed in more detail in *The Rhythms of Strategy, page 34.*) It is also worth noting that strategy is a largely creative activity; planning is a largely logical task. (The creative nature of strategy is explored in *Recognize Strategy As A Creative Act; Unask the Question, page 40.*)

A Goal Is Not The Same As A Strategy

A strategy defines how you will win. Some confuse goals with strategies. Measures of success are necessary (see *Strategy Requires A Value Measure, page 28*), but goals such as "75% market share by 2020" or "Being the most successful car manufacturer in the world" do not constitute a strategy, as they do not address the 'how' question.

Some goal-oriented statements, like GE's famous goal to be number one or number two in the marketplaces they play in, muddy the waters a little, in that whilst the focus on being number one or number two sounds like a goal, it also implies winning through portfolio selection, scale and market power.

The Business World Is Suffering From A Tyranny Of Execution

In the world of business, execution has ended up as a dominant narrative. If you distil out the subtext in most boardrooms and executive committees, you will hear something like "*We need to tick the strategy box, but really execution is what wins the day.*"[2] Albert Einstein neatly summed the situation up with his quote: "A perfection of means, and confusion of aims, seems to be our main problem."

This denigration of strategy creates a double problem for those who (rightly) take strategy seriously. Firstly, there is the obvious and direct issue that strategy discussions and communications often receive short shrift from senior leaders, because communications and discussions about strategy are deemed less important than operational discussions (even if no-one would ever admit to that openly).

Secondly, because of this bias, those that have risen to the top in any organization are typically those that are good at execution, and naturally favour, understand and support those who speak the same language and think the same way as them.

It is hard to change a culture that does not respect strategy, because the effects of good or bad strategy cannot always be felt immediately, whereas the effects of good or bad operational execution can usually be seen almost immediately.

The good news is that those companies, countries, governments, teams and individuals who consistently respect strategy are much more likely to win over time.

---

[2] This reminds me of the equally wrong myth that "*ideas are ten a penny*". In fact, bad ideas are 'ten a penny', good ideas are rare, and great ideas are worth their weight in gold.

Mission And Vision Led Us The Business World Astray

In the world of business, we have been trying to make the formalism of mission and vision statements work for a long time now. The truth is – they are an awful way to frame strategy. Many people can't remember the difference between mission and vision. Many companies use them in opposite ways. The addition of value proposition and strategic intent don't help much either. Trash this language, and instead just use:

* Where we will play
* How we will win[3]
* What capabilities we will need

---

[3] The notion of winning makes it sounds like there is an opponent. As stated earlier, strategy is equally applicable where there is no opponent. But I have stuck with the language of winning here, because it is so brief and clear.

We Are In The Thrall Of Ancient Strategy Texts

We constantly refer back to old strategy texts, particularly those created for the context of war, such as Sun Tzu's "The Art of War". In fact, the etymological roots of the word strategy itself are in the role of a General commanding an army.

This is very limiting, since these military texts often assume the primary challenge is the overcoming of an adversary[4], whereas in fact, the adversarial/ competitive aspects of strategy are often by no means the most important challenges in business, personal or even gaming and sporting contexts. And, in fact, whilst war is a terrible place to be, strategy during wartime is arguably easier than strategy during peacetime – goals are often clearer and less complex, and available resources are more apparent.

---

[4] Some authors have tried to reinterpret military strategy texts to generalize the 'enemy' to mean any obstacle, e.g. R.L. Wing's translation of Sun Tzu's "The Art of War" as "The Art of Strategy". Whilst these works are often quite interesting and surface some good learnings, it is a very twisted way to handle strategy. It is reminiscent of religious astronomers trying to keep the earth at the centre of the universe with more and more convoluted theories, when the better answer was to accept that the earth revolves around the sun.

What Strategy Really Is

Strategy Is One of Three Domains

For any entity, there are three domains. The uppermost is the spiritual-ontological – the domain of meaning and goals. Who are we? What do we exist for? What is our purpose? The middle is the strategic-tactical[5] – the domain of direction and decisions. How will we win? The lowermost is the operational – the domain of actions and behaviours. How do we act? The answer to the spiritual-ontological question may be distilled into a set of values. The answer to the strategic-tactical question may be distilled into a set of principles. The answer to the operations question may be distilled into a set of procedures. The interface between the spiritual-ontological and the strategic-tactical domains is the decision as to 'where we will play'. The interface between the strategic-tactical and the operational is the 'strategic plan'. More generally, each domain guides the one below it: the spiritual-ontological guides the strategic- tactical, and the strategic- tactical drives the operational. But there is also a backpath: the operational realities inform the strategy, through internal capabilities (what we are capable of) and external opportunities and threats (e.g. gaps in the market, competitors' weaknesses). The strategic possibilities similarly inform the spiritual domain. These three domains map well to the heaven-earth-man trinity in East Asian philosophy (heaven = spiritual-ontological, man = strategic-tactical, earth = operational).

---

[5] As discussed in *Strategy And Tactics, page 22*, there is no formal line between strategy and tactics – strategy tends to be larger scale/ slower cycle, tactics smaller scale/ faster cycle

There Is Only One Strategy

For any entity, there is *only one strategy*. There may be many substrategies, many tactics employed, many projects, many activities, many operations. But any entity can only have one top level strategy. For example:

- I will design a martial art that is the most direct and efficient form of defence. (This could be how Bruce Lee thought of the martial art he created - Jeet Kune Do.)
- We provide the lowest cost groceries in Sweden.
- We learn and adapt to our customers' needs faster than anyone else.

Every entity can have only one strategy. In fact, that is one way of defining an entity; a set of resources and capabilities applied to achieve a strategy.

Strategy Is About Success

It is most useful to define strategy as *the discipline of success. How to win*. How to succeed. How to maximize value, happiness or other desirable condition. Successful strategies result in getting more than expected through brute force alone, and more than other strategies, in a given context, with a given value measure.

Strategy Is About Choice

The discipline of strategy helps us make good *choices*. Where we have no choices, we have no need for strategy. Where we have choices, we have need for a strategy. Strategy is no more, and no less, than *the discipline of making good choices in order to succeed.*

The book, The Discipline of Market Leaders, By Treacy and Wiersema, talks about three disciplines (customer intimacy, product leadership, operational excellence) and the importance of being good enough at all three of them, but seeking to excel in one. This is a clear framing of strategy as choice.

Some authorities on strategy, such as Kenichi Ohmae, who wrote "The Mind of The Strategist", have stated that there is only a need for strategy where there is an enemy, or competitors. This is plain wrong (or to be more generous, a different, more limiting, and less useful definition of strategy, which we might call competitive strategy). Strategy applies, and should be applied, whenever there is choice.

Strategy Is Focus

Making lots of good choices is no guarantee of success. Just like winning lots of battles is no guarantee of winning the war. Perhaps the predominant component of a strategy is *focus*. We must avoid being *scattered*. This can be framed as having a strategic posture – an answer the question "how do we set out to win?" It includes both where and how to invest our resources. All choices should then be made in that context. We may choose to lose some battles to win the war. Not every value creating (e.g. Net Present Value[6] positive) investment is a good investment. In fact, the temptation of lots of small, value creating investments that are not aligned with our strategic direction may be seen as a series of breadcrumbs, tempting us off our strategic path. The job of the leadership is to resist that temptation, to keep us laser-focused on our strategic path. (Except for a little *unstrategy* – described later in *Build In Some Unstrategy, page 71.*)

In the world of personal development, the idea of identifying and fixing your weaknesses is on the wane at present, being replaced by the idea of identifying and amplifying your strengths. This is consistent with the notion of focus. We don't have to stick to our current strategic focus forever, but as discussed in *Latching Strategy In, page 33*, we need to latch a strategy in for a while, and use that to prune the tree of possibilities.

---

[6] Net Present Value (NPV) is a way of measuring the financial value of an enterprise or an initiative based on expected cashflows over time, adjusting for the effects of time and risk.

Strategy As Meaning And Motivation

Thinking of strategy as focus, as a means of selecting and prioritizing activities consistently, is accurate and powerful, but also somewhat dry and scientific. A complementary cultural-anthropological-tribal view is strategy as meaning.

Viktor Frankl, an inspirational author and psychotherapist who helped both fellow inmates and guards in Nazi concentration camps, developed logotherapy, a psychotherapeutic method based on finding your meaning; your purpose. It is neatly summarized in the phrase "If you have a *why*, you can live with almost any *how*".

Strategy is one way of expressing the meaning of an individual, company or country. If a company seeks to provide "the highest quality shoes in the world", "the lowest cost groceries in your town", or "an endless stream of highly innovative home appliances that delight the customer", that provides it, its staff, and its customers with a clear sense of what it means, as well as its strategic direction. Viewing strategy as meaning is the interface between the strategic domain and the spiritual-ontological domain described in *Strategy Is One Of Three Domains, page 16.*

This view is not only a philosophical perspective; it has practical applications. While the focus-prioritization perspective might lead to a very detailed, nuanced expression of strategy, the meaning perspective leads us to create a very simple strategy, a meme, a totem pole for the tribe to dance around. An old colleague of mine, Roger Woolfe, was fond of saying "It is better to be really clear and nearly right, than nearly clear and really right." This is not true in all contexts, but it is often true for strategy.

Strategy Plays Within Boundaries And With Boundaries

Strategy works on two levels – firstly how to work what we have got (assets, people, capabilities, products) in the places that we play already. For a sports shoe company selling in the US, this means how to be a successful sports shoe company in the US. For a person who is an accountant, this means how to be a successful accountant.

The second level is whether and how we should change the game – change what we have got, and change where we play. For the shoe company, it might mean a move into sports-related healthcare. For the accountant, it might mean a move into financial trading.

It is useful to refer to this as playing *within* boundaries and playing *with* boundaries.[7]. This is also referred to as working *in* the business, and working *on* the business.[8]

Douglas Hofstadter talks about a related concept, "Jumping Out Of The System" (JOOTSing), in his wonderful tour-de-force on artificial intelligence and other things, "Gödel, Escher Bach: An Eternal Golden Braid".

A complete strategy must address both playing within boundaries and playing with boundaries.

---

[7] This language comes from James Carse's excellent book "Finite and Infinite Games"

[8] From Michael Gerber's "The E-Myth".

Strategy And Tactics

Depending on your perspective, you may label a particular issue as more strategic (big, long-term etc.) or more tactical (small, short-term etc.) There is no fundamental difference between these two – it is a matter of perspective/ opinion. They are both about optimization. It can be useful to use the term strategy and strategic to refer to playing with boundaries, and tactics/ tactical as playing within boundaries. For a company's head of production, the introduction of a 'just-in-time' methodology to radically reduce inventory may seen as highly strategic, whereas the board of directors may view it as important, but a tactical move supporting a low price/ high customer value strategy.

Also, when we think of tactics, we may think a little more about stratagems (see *Strategy And Stratagems, page 23.*)

Strategy And Stratagems

A *stratagem* is a tactic, or trick, designed to confuse or deceive the enemy. Stratagems are mostly used where there is an enemy or one or more competitors, but they can also be used to trick oneself – e.g. dietary stratagems to trick your body into being less hungry. The Chinese classic "thirty six stratagems" is one of the best references on the different types of stratagem.

In executing strategies, we may use stratagems, and strategies give the purpose and guiderails for using stratagems – but strategies are not mainly about stratagems. Strategies are mainly about focus.

It is essential not to be seduced by, or addicted to, stratagems. Amateur players of board games often get sucked into creating the opportunity to execute a 'clever' stratagem (such as sacrificing the queen in chess), and lose the big picture. Similarly, young sportspeople may see professionals executing neat tricks (like a back-heel in football). More advanced players take advantage of that tendency if they observe it in their opponents.

Although it is not a perfect match, it may also be useful to think of strategy more like a game of perfect information such as chess (where nothing is hidden[9]), whereas stratagems are more like a game like poker (where things are hidden).

---

[9] Although no chess pieces are hidden, whereas cards in poker are hidden, it is really a bit simplistic to say nothing is hidden in games of perfect information, since the plans and knowledge in the minds of the players are hidden.

The Components Of Strategy

Strategy Requires Consideration Of The Inside, The Outside And The Options

Deciding on a strategy requires consideration of internal context and capabilities, external opportunities and threats, and the options available to you. In some cases, all the 'action' may seem to be in the external considerations, such as complex competitive dynamics between companies and brands, such as Coke and Pepsi. In other cases we get lost in the internal context; a good example is the period of integration after a merger between two companies. In some cases, for example a chess game, the options available are relatively clear and limited. In other cases, there may be a massive number of options. In still other cases, the options are hard to discern[10]. It is essential that we consider all three (inside, outside, options), and connect them.

---

[10] In the social sciences, one condition that makes something a 'wicked problem' is the lack of a clearly defined set of options.

Strategy Connects The Demand And Supply Sides

Strategy must connect the demand side (where we will play and how we will win) with the supply side (how we will evolve our resources, capabilities, products and services in order to meet those demand side goals). One of the purposes of innovation is to evolve the supply side to more closely meet the demand side. As a simple example, from a demand perspective, it might seem strange to put lots of sick people together in one place (a hospital). From a supply side it makes perfect sense – to achieve economies of scale and scope (efficiency and convenience for medical staff and medical equipment). At the time of writing, technology advances around telemedicine mean that the future may be able to be more focused on the demand side (health, comfort and convenience of the patient). Indeed, one could argue that *progress represents that decoupling of the demand and supply sides*, such that supply side considerations (e.g. patients being physically close to the doctor) constrain the demand side (patients need to get healthy and be comfortable) less and less.

Strategy Requires A Value Measure

In order to create a strategy, you must have a clear picture of how to measure success, or at least how to measure better versus worse. It could be purely about profit. It could be about happiness. It is useful to call the thing we are trying to maximize "*value*". There may be multiple measures of value, but the fewer the better, in order to create focus.

Single-handed round-the-world sailor Pete Goss says that when things got complex in his sailing projects, he would always use the question "What will make the boat go faster?" as a tool to clarify his decision.

It is almost always helpful to be specific about the time nature of the value measure. In some cases, the goal is limited to a defined short-term outcome (e.g. a project's targets, a football game's result). In others it is a balance of short and long-term. In still others the goal is all about long-term value, with a willingness to invest without return in the short and medium terms.

Strategy and Capabilities

The highest level of strategy is the context and strategic posture – where we play and how we win. In order to connect that to supply side strategy (how do we evolve our resources to best support the strategic posture), it is helpful to define the capabilities needed to support the strategic posture. What capabilities do we need as a business or person to allow us to win in the way defined by the strategic posture. For example, a professional fighter who wants to win by tiring out his or her opponent needs to develop the fitness and endurance to do so. A company that wishes to win through closer connection to the customer probably needs the capability to understand its customers better than competitors do.

Strategy Is About Deployment of Resources And Capabilities

The choices we make about strategy govern where and how our resources are used, (particularly our scarcest ones) and which resources we seek to acquire/ develop. In a business context, resources include people, money, physical assets and management time. In a personal context, resources include time, energy, money and relationships. It is helpful to think about the approach to deployment of resources as the supply side of strategy.

The Time Nature of Strategy

Strategy Is About The Future

A strategy is about where we are going, not where we have been. As such, a strategy should mainly focus on the future. Since entities are on a strategic journey, we cannot, however, completely ignore the past and the present. The past, present and future should occupy approximately 10%, 20% and 70% of the time, mindshare and real estate of strategy respectively (unless there is a specific reason to focus more on the past or present.) A strategy should not be an apology for the past.

Saving For The Future Versus Borrowing From The Future

Strategy often depends on trade-offs between value now and value later. Considerations here include how much of our financial and other resources to invest, versus how much to reserve for the future, and also include considering borrowing resources that we don't have, in the expectation that we can repay them later. As much as possible, we should make explicit the way we make decisions about now and future. Identifying where products, business units and assets are in their investment lifecycle is helpful. For example, cash cows is a term often used for things that are profitable now but not expected to grow much more, so yield in the present should be maximized, and investment for the future minimized. Some other opportunities may be seen as future growth opportunities, where investment should be made without expectation of immediate return.

Strategy May Be Defined In Phases

Although strategy should be separate from detailed plans, it may be helpful to identify a few phases of strategy – in order to recognize the expected need to adapt strategy as the entity matures, and the external context changes. This is particularly important in a 'turnaround' context, where immediate strategic focus must be on very tactical issues (e.g. bad contracts, toxic people, outdated practices), but even as we struggle to navigate urgent issues, we must try to make sure we are not mortgaging the future, especially not accidentally and unknowingly. In such situations, it may be an important for a leader to send the dual messages of clear focus on immediate issues, combined with a keen awareness of future potential.

Latching Strategy In

At the time of writing, it is fashionable to talk about emergent strategies, being experimental and democratizing strategy. One might think that the faster a strategy can change, the more agile it is. But the faster it changes, the harder it is for the entity to assimilate and execute on it, and the greater the danger of being scattered and unfocused, confused and sapped of energy and momentum. Changing strategy every day is the same as having no strategy. (In fact it is slightly worse, because you have the illusion of strategy, and waste energy on formulating strategy.) Similarly, strategies that change as frequently as plans are useless. It is most powerful if execution and experimentation takes place within a set of strategic guidelines that last for the medium term.

The Rhythms Of Strategy

All enterprises and individuals have four rhythms– the very short term, the short term, the medium term, and the long term. For a typical company at the time of writing, the very short term is a quarter (3 months), the short term is 1 year, the medium term is 2-3 years, and the long term is 5-10 years.

- The very short term is for monitoring the plan, and tuning it.
- The short term is for refreshing the plan, and tuning the strategy.
- The medium term is for completely refreshing the strategy.

Note that this discussion is about the time nature of strategy creation, not the time periods that are covered in the content of the strategy. In terms of content, both strategy and plan should cover all four periods, in decreasing levels of detail.

Harmonizing With Other Rhythms

Strategy should recognize and attempt to harmonize with the natural rhythms and cycles on the inside and in the external context of the entity. In the case of a company, there is the natural cycle of the company itself, in terms of maturity of processes, need for change and ability to absorb change. There is also the tenure of the CEO and other senior leaders, economic and political cycles of relevant geographies, and maturity of relevant industries. These all represent cycles to be synchronized with.

Good investments are not always at the right time. There is a time to open up possibilities, a time to close down on returns. The Taoist concept of *tao* is helpful here – trying to observe and go with the flow. Also, the financial notion of *duration* of investments (a measure of their time nature) is helpful.

How To Create Strategy

Strategy Should Be Formulated In One Very Short Term Quantum

It is possible to discuss and agonize over strategy for ages. This doesn't benefit the company. Having a strategy in place, even if it is not absolutely optimal, is more powerful than agonizing over the best strategy for years. As a rule of thumb, try to limit the creation of the strategy to one very short term quantum – in a corporate case, that is typically three months. (See *The Rhythms Of Strategy, page 34*.) Strategy and plan may take two quanta to formulate, especially in a large, multi-entity enterprise, but if they can both be done in one quantum, all the better.

Treat Strategy As A Tribal Conversation, Not A Scientific Project

It is tempting to think of strategy as a scientific discipline. When we think of strategy creation as a project, we get a few smart people in a room to analyse and synthesize, with occasional touch-points with the outside world. But strategy is about getting groups of people to behave in particular, focused ways; it is more helpful to think of strategy as an anthropological, or tribal, discipline, as described in *Strategy As Meaning And Motivation, page 20*. The concrete effect of this thinking is to make sure strategy is simple enough for everyone to understand, and to invest more in innovative communications and interventions to engage all stakeholders throughout the strategy creation process. Strategy should be treated as a narrative –a conversation more than a project. Its success depends on its *liquidity* (how much it is flowing round the enterprise/ ecosystem) as much as its accuracy. This is related to the social science notions of Wicked Problems and Social Messes. (See *Useful Reference Work, page 79*.)

Strategy And Anti-Strategy

Many strategies suffer from the 'alpha male, chest beating' problem, of simply stating how great we will be, and how we will succeed. This is not enough. If strategy represents a focus (how we will win) guiding a series of choices, we should be able to state the focuses we are not taking, and the choices we are discarding. A great strategy throws its focus and choices into stark relief by articulating its anti-strategy. This is the combination of substance and absence creating meaning, just like the light and dark shades in a painting; the notes and the pauses in music, and the walls and the empty space inside containers that in combination make them useful.

The anti-strategy should outline focuses and choices that could be valid aspects of a similar entity's strategy, but are not ours.

It is a great discipline to ensure every single statement in a strategy represents a choice, by writing it as a strategy/anti-strategy pair. For example, "We will centralize and standardize every business process considered a commodity; we will not allow business units complete autonomy".

Applying The Strategic Razor

Strategies often suffer from *strategic bloat* – strategy documents and communications being way too long, and padded out with useless stuff. Go through every line of your strategy, and check if each statement has a valid alternative (anti-strategy). If it doesn't, throw it out, since it doesn't represent a choice, and hence has no place in a strategy. It may belong elsewhere, such as a set of values, or an operating manual, just not in a strategy. Occam's Razor is a useful notion here – "the simplest answer is the best", tempered by Einstein's famous warning "Everything should be made as simple as possible, but not simpler".

Recognize Strategy As A Creative Act; Unask The Question

Planning is a largely logical activity; strategy is largely a creative act. This has a number of implications. First, in a company, it is likely that different people are needed to lead strategy and planning. For personal strategy, you have to lead both activities yourself, although you may want to seek help or advice for either or both. Also, it is important to sit with the strategy questions a while, try to reframe them, and get creative input, before leaping to a solution.

There is an elegant concept from Zen Buddhism, called *MU* – unask the question[11]. It means that you should not let yourself be captured by a dumb or sub-optimal question. For example, the best question may not be how to enter China, but whether to enter China. The best question may not be how to sell more, but how to maximize profit.

---

[11] From the Zen Buddhist 'riddle' Joshu's dog, in the book Mumonkan.

Use Frameworks; Don't Let Them Use You

Those who have studied strategy or business in general will have been exposed to many frameworks. Examples include Michael Porter's five forces, McKinsey's seven 'S' framework and the Boston Consulting Group's Growth-Share matrix. Frameworks can be helpful in rendering the complex simple. Frameworks are particularly helpful if they hold the property of being 'MECE' – mutually exclusive and collectively exhaustive. What this means is that they cover the entire space under consideration (CE), and the pieces don't overlap (ME) – like a perfectly fitting jigsaw. Three notes of caution regarding use of frameworks:

- Frameworks are not the truth. Like all abstract theory, frameworks are a way to think of things. They are not the only way, and they are unlikely to be a perfect representation of reality. Use them as long as they are useful.

- Frameworks are not neutral[12]. Breaking things down into the pieces of a framework feels neutral, but inevitably, it is imposing a particular view. It may, for example, give a bias to physical rather than intangible assets, or assume the customer only interacts with the company at the end of the supply chain. Be vigilant about the assumptions and biases inherent in each framework you use.

- Frameworks may expire, or require updating. The world changes, and we have to make sure our frameworks still apply. For example, the world of technology and the Internet has made platform and ecosystem effects (delivering value together) more important – these ecosystem relationships are not well captured by linear value chain frameworks.

---

[12] Inspired by the philosopher Jacques Derrida's saying, "deconstruction is not neutral".

Learn From The Past, But Don't Be Enslaved By It

George Santayana's wonderful quote "Those who cannot remember the past are condemned to repeat it" reminds us that we should be informed by past successes and failures, in order to improve on the past, rather than simply replay it over and over again. Two notes of caution:

First, we should be wary of assigning causality. Just because you exhibited a particular behaviour in the past and you were successful (or failed), that doesn't mean the behaviour caused the success (or failure).

Second, we should ensure we recognize where circumstances have changed, and how that should change our approach. We sometimes see entrepreneurs revert to the behaviours that made them succeed initially, especially when the going gets tough – but those initial success behaviours may not work in their current situation.

Don't Bite Off More Than You Can Chew

What may seem the optimal strategy may be sub-optimal because of *change capacity* – the ability to create and culturally assimilate change. For example, many Merger and Acquisition (M&A) integration strategies adopt a best-of-breed approach – picking and choosing the best of both businesses' processes and systems, then sewing them together. This may be optimal in theory, but it ties up the enterprise in internal navel gazing for too long, and can be too hard to assimilate culturally. Hence, sometimes in M&A it is better to adopt an absorption strategy (use one company's business system, and bring the other company's book of business onto that business system, discarding the other company's business system), accepting losses of functionality and sub-optimization in some areas. There is a related concept in decision science called 'bounded rationality', recognizing the limits of human cognition, and factoring that into decision-making.

Strategy in Large And Complex Organizations

Top-Level Strategy And Sub-Strategies

As discussed in *There Is Only One Strategy, page 17*, every entity has only one top-level strategy. Since every entity that needs to make choices can, and should, have a strategy, business units within a business, functional areas such as marketing, geographic areas and assets should have their own strategies. From an enterprise-wide perspective, these are sub-strategies. Every sub-strategy inherits the strategy for the entity above it, and is built relative to it. So, for example, a business unit strategy inherits the corporate strategy, and adds detail where it is left open at the corporate level, and defines exceptions to the corporate strategy where necessary.

Align Plans; Integrate Sub-Strategies

Plans are separate from strategies, but must be tightly *aligned* with them. Note that the word aligned implies both an 'otherness' (plans are not the same type of thing as strategies) and a subservience (plans are in some sense lesser than strategies).

For sub-strategies, the term alignment is not appropriate. Instead think of integrating sub-strategies into the whole strategy. The sub-strategy is a part of the overall strategy, rather than something other to be aligned to it.

The Backpath From Sub-Strategies

Conventionally, we think of sub-strategies as conceptually and chronologically downstream from entity-wide strategy. For example, in a company, we set high-level corporate strategy, and then we set marketing strategy, human resource strategy and other functional strategies, to help us achieve that corporate strategy. It is important, however, to recognize the backpath from sub-strategies to corporate strategy. So, for example, IT strategy should be defined to enable corporate strategy to be achieved, but informational capabilities may also change the corporate strategy – i.e. it may allow us to get into new businesses, change how we win, make existing businesses/ approaches less attractive etc. We must not ignore the backpaths from sub-strategies.

The Realpolitik Of Strategy

Strategy Requires Courage And Commitment

If a strategy contains real strategic choices, it is almost inevitable that strategy will create disagreement from time to time. A real strategy will almost certainly end up saying no to some opportunities, or ways of doing things. And if a strategy chooses some less easily measurable investments over some more easily measurable ones, because of perceived value, there is an unavoidable need for faith, since choices made cannot be 'proven' in the short term. Also, the implications of strategy almost always cut across multiple functional areas/ business units/ power bases, and typically demand trade-offs that may be sub-optimal from a single power base point of view.

All of this means that following through on a strategy requires both courage and commitment.

Strategy And Signalling

Every action, every communication, every move, has two values – its intrinsic value, and its signalling value. In other words, everything we do, everything we say, every choice we make, sends a signal as to our intent and commitment. For example, when strategy is delegated to a relatively junior employee, or a consultant, this may well be interpreted as a signal that strategy is not very important – because key leaders are not spending their time on it. (Even if the leader is very busy, and the junior employee/ consultant is very skilled.)

Signalling is one of the reasons that we must be careful about outsourcing the creation of strategy. Normally it is acceptable, and often desirable, to out-task specific tasks related to strategy, including mundane tasks (e.g. data collection), tasks that require very specific skills (e.g. real option valuation), and tasks that benefit from independence (e.g. auditing/ checking a strategy), but outsourcing the whole of strategy creation sends very counterproductive signals.

This idea of signalling is very consistent with the earlier discussed idea of strategy as a conversation. It is not only the content of the conversation that is important, but also the style of the conversation and who is having the conversation.

False Signalling

Signalling deliberately designed to confuse or mislead competitors can be valuable. Pretending to be strong where you are weak or weak where you are strong, pretending to focus where you are not focusing and vice versa, can be effective tactics. We see this a lot in feinting in boxing and other combat sports. A related concept is what the Chinese classic 36 stratagems book calls "Beating the Grass To Flush Out The Snake"; sending signals/ taking actions designed to deliberately uncover hidden dangers/ and/or flush out what your competitors are thinking.

Take Strategy The Last Mile In Communication

For strategy to be executed, the hearts, minds and hands of stakeholders must be won. However, they may experience strategy as abstract, boring and/ or not related to their day-to-day reality. A key part of strategy is communicating it in a way that is meaningful to stakeholders, and addresses the "What's in it for me?" question for those stakeholders. Executing on this requires a clear understanding of each major stakeholder/ group, in order to take the messages of strategy the last mile to what they really care about. This includes tailoring content, language, timing and communication style. It may also be helpful to use metaphors and analogies to make abstract concepts more tangible and easily understood.

Use Principles To Increase The Liquidity Of Strategy

Just like a financial currency, strategy is only useful if it is being used day-to-day; if it is liquid. A powerful technique for increasing the liquidity of strategy is to encode the strategy in a short set (8-10) of principles that can be used in making decisions and influencing behaviours. Great principles satisfy three criteria:

1. They are connected to how you succeed - your strategic posture
2. They are specific to your enterprise/ you as a person – not just generic goodness (See section: *Strategy And Anti-Strategy, page 29.*)
3. They are detailed enough to really drive decisions and influence behaviours

Avoid Spurious Accuracy And Unnecessary Information

We have an innate desire for certainty that comes from a fear of the unknown. Hence, everything in strategy should be defined as clearly and as accurately as possible, but no more than that. Don't provide more detail that you can be sure about. Avoid spurious accuracy – it can be dangerous and counterproductive.

A related point is avoiding providing more information in a strategy than necessary. In sales, there is a saying: "Don't sell past the close". Perhaps less snappy, but in strategy, we should remember "Don't inform beyond the strategy" – to keep things as clear and simple as possible.

Important Strategic Concepts

Look For Synergies

We all have limited resources at our disposal, and even if we have infinite resources (although we rarely do; there is almost always a bottleneck), we wish to use those resources efficiently. One very powerful way of achieving strategic efficiency is looking for synergies – moves which have multiple meanings/ sources of value.

Two common synergy effects are economies of scale - being able to do things cheaper due to the volume of stuff you are doing, and economies of scope - being able to use resources for multiple activities, e.g. a shared service centre can serve multiple business units.

Synergies can come from any asset or capability, including factories (that can make multiple product lines), sales channels (that can sell multiple products/ services), product components (that can be used in multiple products), customer relationships, brands and information.

There is also a more abstract version of economies of scope – doing things for multiple reasons. In turn-based games, such as chess or go, where players get to alternate, synergies are a way to go faster – achieving multiple things with one move. Wing Chun Kung Fu encompasses the synergy concept of a combined defensive-attacking manoeuvre – why block when you can block-and-punch in one move?

Make Leveraged Moves

A more general concept than synergy - *leverage* is the important capability to create a relatively large impact through a relatively small effort or change. Leverage frees us from resource intensity, so value created by your entity can grow faster than value consumed by it. Just for example, investing in a piece of technology that makes every sales person more efficient is a more leveraged move than hiring a new salesperson.

Distinguish Between Commodities And Differentiators

It is helpful to separate services, processes and capabilities into commodities and differentiators. Commodities are things you have to do, but are not real sources of success. They are 'tickets to the game'. All things being equal, commodities should be ruthlessly standardized, simplified, probably centralized, maybe outsourced – to minimize cost for a given level of risk and quality. Differentiators are what make you win.

Strategy And Agility

Agility is the ability to change quickly, cheaply and safely, in the ways that one is likely to need to change. Agility is not the same as flexibility. Flexibility is expensive and makes change harder. Part of agility is working out where you need to be flexible and where you don't. Ruthless simplification of commodities and rich flexibility in differentiators is typically the way to maximize agility.

Strategy And Complexity

Unnecessary complexity is bad. In general, complexity in commodities is bad unless it is essential to serve differentiated needs. Complexity in differentiators may be good if it helps you win, e.g. by servicing customer needs better, we may make it harder for competitors to compete with us.

In a competitive context, you may choose to create external (market) complexity if you think you can deal with it better than a competitor. i.e. Muddying the waters may be worse for a competitor than for you. In short – *any complexity that exists should be deliberate, not accidental.*

The Value Of Options

Part of strategy is giving yourself choices. One way of looking at how well a society is doing is how much choice its citizens have. In finance, there are very sophisticated formulas to price the option of being able to do something (e.g. buy stocks at a specific price for a given period). Common sense makes us think that options only have value when they are exercised, but just like insurance should not be considered a waste even if you don't need to use it, holding options has value. Hence increasing your options is a smart strategic move. Borrowing from the board game Go, we should try to make flexible shapes that can evolve differently depending on future context. An associated advanced concept from Go is *yosu miru* – causing an adversary to become less flexible – to fix their direction. (Contrast this with *The Value Of Limiting Options, page 64.*)

Strategy And Uncertainty

In the real world, strategy has to be conducted in uncertain contexts – uncertainty about how the environment will evolve (the unknowable), and also about hidden information, such as competitors' financials, plans and motivations (the unknown). Techniques such as articulating your assumptions, performing sensitivity analyses and scenario planning help with the unknowable. Competitive intelligence helps to minimize the unknown.

Strategy And Risk

We might fantasize that having a great strategy insulates us from risk. In fact, strategic thinking about risk should be much more sophisticated than trying to eliminate all risk. The engineering view of risk is that all risk is bad, and in an ideal world we get rid of it. A strategic view of risk is closer to the way the financial industry thinks of risk. It is inefficient to invest only in completely safe, certain, known arenas. We must take risks, but look to manage risks, and ensure that all our activities are not contingent on one risk – but instead diversify our portfolio of activities. So, for example, our whole strategy should not be dependent on the fortunes of one currency or one commodity.

Pete Goss is a round-the-world sailor and adventurer, who use his sailing and other experiences to illustrate a talk on leadership. He has been accused of being a daredevil risk-taker, but using arguments about tests he does before a race/ adventure, he points out that he does not take risk; he embraces it.

Advanced Strategy Concepts

The Highest Form Of Winning Is Win-Winning

In many martial arts, the founders make the point that the best way to win a fight is by not being there, or by somehow dispelling the aggression without fighting. Similarly, the highest form of winning is by identifying a way to win that doesn't make others (such as customers and competitors) lose. So, for example, creating a product that has more value to customers and charging them a little more is better than simply charging more because you can. This win-winning is often achieved by finding what economists call 'deadweight losses' – where an unhelpful equilibrium is reached. For example, if the minimum wage is set too high in a country, there will be people who want to work who can't get a job, and people who want to employ them who can't afford to. Lowering the minimum wage in that case unlocks a bunch of value for everyone.

Ways of win-winning include:

- Segmenting customers more accurately, so they can be served more exactly with what they need
- Creating 'blue oceans', serving a need that was never previously served, either because it has only just become possible, or because it was overlooked
- Specializing rather than competing. As economist David Ricardo pointed out, comparative advantage is better for everyone than competitive advantage. If we can focus on what we are relatively good at, and make space for others to focus on what they are relatively good at, it is much better than us all doing the same things.

Exploiting Platformization Effects

The notion of building on previous work in order to create more value runs throughout history. The phrase "standing on the shoulders of giants" was used by Isaac Newton[13] to note that his discoveries and inventions built on ideas of earlier scientists. In computer science, the notion of metalinguistic abstraction refers to creating a powerful language that deals with a particular problem domain, which can then be used to solve problems. This idea of a 'platformization effect' – creating a platform that can then be built on, is powerful in strategy too. We have seen it recently in the world of computers and the Internet, where platforms, such as Apple's iTunes, create the ability for others to build on and add value to a product or service. Platforms can reduce time-to-market, increase value-add and customer switching costs.

Strategists should consider platform effects when designing their enterprise's strategy. What platforms could be leveraged by us? What platforms threaten us? What platforms could/ should we build?

---

[13] The phrase Newton used was "If I have seen further, it is by standing on the shoulders of giants". Apparently the notion of standing on the shoulders of giants was first used in the 12th century by Bernard of Chartres.

The Value Of Limiting Options

In contrast to *The Value Of Options, page 58*, sometimes it can be valuable to limit our options. There are at least two good reasons to do this.

1. To signal commitment – hence the stories of commanders burning their boats, burning bridges etc. so there is no turning back.
2. To make decision making manageable. Psychologists talk about bounded rationality. There is a limit to how much analysis we can do. On a similar note, the book "The Paradox of Choice" highlighted the fact that more choice can make us less happy, especially where we have limited information/ ability to make the choice.

As discussed in *Strategy And Complexity, page 58*, a sophisticated idea related to this is to create complexity that requires choices that we are more able to make than our competitors. Metaphorically, taking your enemy into deep, foggy waters, where you are more able to navigate than them.

Understand Lightness And Heaviness

When taking an action, such as making a move in a board game, or a company releasing a product, or a person entering a relationship, it is important to be clear as to whether you are doing that 'heavily' or 'lightly'. Heavy moves are the cornerstones of the strategic edifice you are building, and should be backed up with strong support and commitment. Light moves are executed for specific tactical reasons, but may not need to be defended. One type of light move is a false signal designed to mislead an opponent. (Discussed in *False Signalling, page 52*.) Experiments, from which we learn and adapt, are another. A third category is moves designed to disrupt an opponent, rather than for us to get profit. In the game of Go, this concept of lightness is known as *sabaki*.

When we are executing light moves, we must be flexible, and be willing to sacrifice and change shape. I like to think of lizards that are willing to shed their tail in order to escape. In light situations, nothing is sacred other than the general intent. This is highly related to the notion of sunk costs, discussed in *Recognize Sunk Costs, page 70*.

The Value Of Not Making A Move

Implicit in the way we think about strategy, games, competitions etc. is the idea that taking an action, making a decision, playing a move, sending a signal, is always powerful, and that whenever we have the chance to make a decision or take an action, we should. In fact, that is not always the case. In the world of chess, there is a lovely use of the German word *zugzwang*, describing the predicament of being obliged to make a move, when one would be better off not moving.

More generally, the Taoist notion of *wu wei* (not doing), points us to the value of light-touch strategy, management and leadership, observing the natural flow, and taking only small corrective actions. In the primary Taoist text, Tao Te Ching, chapter 60, Lao Tzu manages to combine the absurd with the insightful in his statement *"Ruling the country is like cooking a small fish; it should be done lightly."*

The value of not doing should be taken into consideration when creating and executing on strategy. Some companies have found value in changing the 'do nothing' option from the default if nothing else is chosen, to a peer of other options, that itself has to have a business case.

Play Away From Strength (But Not Too Far)

Although strategy is about focus – hence about playing to your strengths - investing in areas that you are already sufficiently strong in is inefficient. Of course, sufficiently strong is a judgement call, based not just on the present but the anticipated future. Nevertheless, making moves that are a significant stretch from your areas of strength is smart and strategically efficient.

Similarly, in competitive/ adversarial contexts, investing and making moves that are too close to adversaries/ competitor's strengths is dangerous. The overall message – keep your distance from strength, whether yours or a competitor's.

Choosing how far you play away from your and your opponents' strengths is the art.

Learn By Analogy, Not By Hero-Worship

There is often an opportunity to innovate your strategy by learning from other contexts. For example a football team may learn from a cricket team's strategy. Or a telecoms company in one country may learn from one in another. Or – more of a stretch – a bank may learn from a retail chain. The key is to look for learnings in contexts that are structurally similar, not simply hero worshipping successful companies. At the time of writing everyone wants to be like Apple. In the recent past, companies we all want to be like included Nokia, Samsung, Sony, GE, Nintendo and ABB. Learnings from structurally similar companies tend to be much more reliably applicable to our context.

Kill Your Own Ghosts

The martial artist Bruce Lee said that "The best thing we can do for our children is to kill our own ghosts". Avoid obsession with competitors, regulations, or any other one aspect of strategy. In the book "The Unfettered Mind", a collection of three letters from Zen master Takuan Soho to sword master Yagyu Munenori, Takuan talks about a custom of hanging a painting of a mythical beast Pai Che to eat bad dreams and misfortune. He states that "When a house does not have a painting of a Pai Che, it is like having no ghosts at all." Also in "The Unfettered Mind", Takuan uses the symbolism of a one-thousand armed deity (Kannon), making the point that if you allow your mind to be focused on any one arm, the other nine hundred and ninety nine are useless.

The bottom line is that we have to identify and eliminate our obsessions, since they will stop us making balanced strategic decisions.

Don't Dance To The Tune Of Competitors

A specific instance of 'killing our own ghosts' relates to competitors. Whilst we have to be vigilant and aware of competitors' activities, an over obsession on competition, or even worse on one particular competitor, effectively gives control of the game to them, allowing them to control and manipulate us. This is related to the psychological concept of 'anchoring' – setting the parameters for a dialogue or negotiation.

Being obsessed with beating competition in general may make you miss the opportunity to enter a completely different space. A related concept, outlined in the "The Book of Five Rings" by Miyamoto Musashi, is "Rat's Head, Ox's Neck". Musashi encourages the reader to refuse to engage in the way the competitor wants to, and deliberately change the nature of the 'dialog' – Rat's Head being very detailed, Ox's Neck very broad brush.

Recognize Sunk Costs

Avoid being driven by past investment decisions. Just because you have invested in something, doesn't mean you should continue to. Decisions should be based on value from a today and tomorrow perspective, not yesterday.

Of course, this perspective can be very politically challenging, as no-one likes to be responsible for, or accept, failures. Hence no-one likes to have their project killed. There is massive value in being prepared and able to kill or radically change badly performing investments, no matter how much investment has already been put in.

A counterpoint to this is the willingness to go back to areas of previous failure. At the time of writing, Apple's commercial failure with the Newton handheld device lies in stark contrast to the success of the iPad.

Build in Some Unstrategy

The vast majority of the time, attention, resources, projects, operations of an organization should be aligned with the strategic focus of the organization. That is the power of strategic focus and momentum. But there is also a danger – of stagnation and strategic blind spots. In order to ensure the organization keeps growing, and there are no strategic blind spots, a significant minority of time attention and resources should go on *unstrategic* activities – experimenting with new things, running different kinds of business etc, in order to learn and facilitate change over time. Note that this is not the same as saying some resources should be spent on experimentation and innovation – most innovation work should be guided by strategy. Every enterprise is different, but aiming for about 90% strategic work, 10% unstrategic work is quite a good rule of thumb.

Relationship of Strategy To Other Disciplines

Strategy Is Only One Management System

A *management system* is a way to lead and manage an organization. Strategy is one. Organization Structure is one. Governance is one. Leadership is another. There are more. It is helpful to think of management systems in a compensatory relationship. It is impossible to make each management system perfect on its own; there are always compromises. But in combination, management systems can create the perfect outcome.

Strategy And Leadership

Leadership is the discipline of influencing external stakeholders to help the entity you are leading to succeed, and inspiring internal stakeholders to higher levels of performance within the guidelines set down by the strategy. Strategy and leadership work hand-in-hand. Strategy defines the purpose which leadership is used to execute on, and leadership is used to help create the right strategy, and ensure its execution.

Strategy without leadership is impotent; Leadership without strategy is meaningless[14].

---

[14] This is reminiscent of the Sex Pistols lyric "Don't know what I want, but I know how to get it" in the song "Anarchy in the UK".

Strategy And Governance

Governance is the discipline of monitoring and making decisions. Governance is achieved in many ways, including the use of committees, financial management mechanisms, principles and metrics. Governance should be designed for each type of decision/ monitoring. Strategy is one domain of governance – there must be a mechanism for deciding governance. Many people think governance is strategy-neutral – i.e. good governance is good governance whatever the enterprise's strategy is. In fact, the way we make decisions must be aligned with our strategic posture. For example, when a company's dominant strategy is to drive revenue growth through highly customized offerings, it is likely that many domains of governance should be highly decentralised. On the other hand, when the goal is to minimize cost and complexity to win through superior profitability, it is likely that most governance should be highly centralized.

Hence strategy influences the design of governance, and governance is used to create strategy. Strategy and governance co-create each other, like the two hands drawing each other in the famous M.C. Escher picture.

Strategy And Culture

In a company or other group context, there is a culture – values, social habits, norms etc. Peter Drucker once famously commented "culture eats strategy for breakfast". In other words, if the culture doesn't accept the strategy, the strategy will not be followed. Cultures are slippery, intangible things, hard to get hold of, and slow to change. Hence effective strategy creation and implementation must involve understanding and working with the culture, evangelizing and embedding the strategy in the culture.

Strategy And Politics

Every enterprise has internal tensions and power struggles that make setting an entity-wide focus hard. These include agency problems (members of the entity having motives and incentives that differ from the entity as a whole), and parts of the entity having different needs from the entity as a whole. This concept even applies to an individual person, who has multiple needs and motivations that may conflict with each other.

Hence being a successful strategist requires careful consideration of power and politics.

Strategy And Values/ Ethics/ Morals/ Religion

As noted in *Strategy Is One Of Three Domains, page 16*, strategy sits in the centre of a three-domain world: Spiritual/ Ontological, Strategic/Tactical, and Operational.

Our ethics, morals, religion – our higher purpose – sits in the spiritual/ ontological domain, but guides strategy by defining what we consider to be value – hence the metric we are trying to maximize with strategy. It also sets boundaries for what we will and won't consider – for example, cheating in sport. It is powerful if our higher beliefs are encoded in a relatively short (8-10) set of values, that can be used to ensure the strategy is optimizing on the right variable, and not stepping outside our boundaries. Values are about what we hold dear and inviolable. Note that values are not the same as principles (described in *Use Principles To Increase The Liquidity Of Strategy, page 53.*)

Useful
Reference
Works

Title:	Strategy Safari: A Guided Tour Through the Wilds of Strategic Management
Author(s):	Henry Mintzberg, Bruce Ahlstrand, and Joseph Lampel
Identifying info:	ASIN: B00HK2UV4G
Reasons it's here:	A really good summary of a lot of the academic work on strategy.

Title:	The Only Sustainable Edge
Author(s):	John Hagel and John Seely Brown
Identifying info:	ISBN-13: 978-1599040660
Reasons it's here:	An interesting book that purports that the only source of sustainable advantage comes from the ability to learn better and faster than others. They coin the lovely term "productive friction".

Title:	Competitive Advantage
Author(s):	Michael E. Porter
Identifying info:	ISBN-13: 978-0029250907
Reasons it's here:	A classic book from Michael Porter, who may view as having a pre-eminent place in modern business strategy.

Title:	Finite and Infinite Games
Author(s):	James P. Carse
Identifying info:	ISBN-13: 978-1476731711
Reason it's here:	A magical book that defies categorization. My favourite book of all time. Referenced in *Strategy Plays Within Boundaries And With Boundaries, page 21*

Title:	The Mind of the Strategist: The Art of Japanese Business
Author(s):	Kenichi Ohmae
Identifying info:	ISBN-13: 978-0140091281
Reasons it's here:	An interesting book on competitive strategy by a leading practitioner, one time head o McKinsey in Japan. Referenced in *Strategy Is About Choice*, *page 18*.
Title:	The Art of Strategy: A Game Theorist's Guide to Success in Business and Life
Author(s):	Avinash K. Dixit and Barry J. Nalebuff
Identifying info:	ISBN-13: 978-0393062434
Reasons it's here:	An interesting book about applying game theory to strategic decision making.
Title:	The Discipline of Market Leaders: Choose Your Customers, Narrow Your Focus, Dominate Your Market
Author(s):	Michael Treacy and Fred Wiersema
Identifying info:	ISBN-13: 978-0201406481
Reasons it's here:	A book that clearly exposes strategy as choice, in the corporate world. Referenced in *Strategy Is About Choice*, *page 18*.

Title:	Winning
Author(s):	Jack Welch with Suzy Welch
Identifying info:	ISBN-13: 978-0061240171
Reasons it's here:	A concise book on strategy without the academic frills by the ex-CEO of GE. GE is seen as one of the most successful and disciplined exponents of strategy management practices in the last few decades.
Title:	Playing to Win
Author(s):	A.G. Lafley
Identifying info:	ISBN-13: 978-0007197699
Reasons it's here:	A clear book about strategy by the CEO of Procter and Gamble, an iconic retail company at the time of writing, with a view of strategy very compatible with the approach taken in this book. Lafley was also advised by Peter Drucker, a famous management expert.
Title:	Essential Drunker
Author(s):	Peter Drunker
Identifying info:	ISBN-13: 978-0750685061
Reasons it's here:	Peter Drunker is a great thinker on management. Worth a read.
Title:	Do More Great Work
Author(s):	Michael Bungay-Stanier
Identifying info:	ISBN-13: 978-0761156444
Reasons it's here:	A little bit peripheral to strategy, but a great little book on how to make time for what truly matters,

Title: Strategy as a Wicked Problem (article)
Author(s):   John C. Camillus
Identifying info: Harvard Business Review, May 2008
Reasons it's here: Takes the notion of wicked problems, and applies it to the domain of strategy. The ideas of wicked problems and social massages come from easier works of Horst Rittel and Robert Horn, amongst others. Referenced in *Treat Strategy As A Tribal Conversation, Not A Scientific Project, page 38.*

Title: Strategy Maps: Converting Intangible Assets into Tangible Outcomes
Author(s):   Robert S. Kaplan and David P. Norton
Identifying info: ISBN-13: 978-1422163498
Reasons it's here: From the creators of the balanced scorecard, the methodology outlined here has become very popular, although it is much more about planning than strategy.

Title: The E-Myth Revisited: Why Most Small Businesses Don't Work and What To Do About It
Author(s):   Michael Gerber
Identifying info: ISBN-13: 978-0887307287
Reasons it's here: Highlights the difference between 'working IN the business' and 'working ON the business'. Referenced in *Strategy Plays Within Boundaries And With Boundaries, page 21.*

Title:	The Paradox of Choice: Why More Is Less
Author(s):	Barry Schwartz
Identifying info:	ISBN-13: 978-0060005696
Reasons it's here:	Referenced in *The Value Of Limiting Options, page 64*, this book explores the notion that more choice is not always good.

Title:	Derrida: A Very Short Introduction (Very Short Introductions)
Author(s):	Simon Glendinning
Identifying info:	ISBN-13: 978-0192803450
Reasons it's here:	An introduction to the ideas of Jacques Derrida, an extremely original thinker, famous for his concept of deconstruction, mentioned in *Use Frameworks; Don't Let Them Use You, page 41*. Derrida's own books are quite inaccessible.

Title:	Tao Te Ching
Author(s):	Lao Tsu, translated by Gia Fu Feng and Jane English
Identifying info:	ISBN-13: 978-0704500075
Reasons it's here:	The definition work of Taoism, Introducing the notion of Tao an Wu Wei referenced in *Harmonizing With Other Rhythms, page 35* and *Understand Lightness And Heaviness, page 65*.

Title:	The Art of War
Author(s):	Sun Tzu, translated by Thomas Cleary
Identifying info:	ISBN-13: 978-1590302255
Reasons it's here:	Perhaps the most famous and iconic classic on military strategy, referenced in *We Are In The Thrall Of Ancient Strategy Texts, page 13*. (There are many translations and versions of this book.)

Title:	The Art of Strategy
Author(s):	Sun Tzu, interpreted by R.L. Wing
Identifying info:	ISBN-13: 978-0385237840
Reasons it's here:	References in *We Are In The Thrall Of Ancient Strategy Texts, page 13*, this is an attempt to translate Sun Tzu's classic Art of War to a more pure strategy context.

Title:	The Thirty-Six Stratagems: A Modern Interpretation Of A Classic (Infinite Success)
Author(s):	Peter Taylor
Identifying info:	ISBN-13: 978-1906821838
Reasons it' here:	One of the best references on the different types of Stratagem that may be applied. Referenced in *Strategy And Stratagems, page 23,* and *False Signalling, page 52*. (There are many translations and versions of this book.)

Title:	The Book of Five Rings
Author(s):	Miyamoto Musashi
Identifying info:	ISBN-13: 978-159039841
Reasons it's here:	A book about winning written by a famously successful Japanese swordsman. Referenced in *Don't Dance To The Tune Of Competitors*, page 69. (There are many translations and versions of this book.)

Title:	The Unfettered Mind
Author(s):	Takuan Soho
Identifying info:	ASIN: B00DO8VPJK
Reasons it's here:	Letters on strategy and stratagems from Zen Master Takuan Soho to sword master Yagyu Munenori. Not that accessible, but some deep stuff worth thinking about in here. Referenced in *Kill Your Own Ghosts, page 68*.

Title:	Gödel, Escher, Bach: An Eternal Golden Braid
Author(s):	Douglas Hofstadter
Identifying info:	ISBN-13: 978-0394756820
Reasons it's here:	The notion of jumping out of the system (JOOTSing), discussed in *Strategy Plays Within Boundaries And With Boundaries, page 21*.

Title: Good Strategy/Bad Strategy: The
                    Difference and Why it Matters
Author(s):   Richard Rumelt
Identifying info: ASIN: B998FHDDJU
Reasons it's here: A popular strategy book at the time of
                    writing, modeling strategy as the trinity
                    of diagnosis, policy, actions.

Title: Strategy: A History
Author(s):   Lawrence Freedman
Identifying info: ISBN-13: 978-0199325153
Reasons it's here: A big book on strategy, with lots of
                    military background.

Cover Art By Amita Jettana

Printed in Great Britain
by Amazon

12316346R00051